Moving Day

FRAGILE

Written by Nicola Barrie ■ Illustrated by Lian Hathaway

We pack the toys
into a box.
We are moving today.

We pack the clothes
into a box.
We are moving today.

We pack the food
into a box.
We are moving today.

We pack the pots
and pans into a box.
We are moving today.

We pack the pictures
into a box.
We are moving today.

We pack the television
into a box.
We are moving today.

We pack the computer
into a box.
We are moving today.

We pack the cat
into a box.
We are moving today.